CHAMBERS HARRAP

GW01112059

PRIMARY
FRENCH
TEACHERS' RESOURCE PACK

Published in Great Britain in 2006
by Chambers Harrap Publishers Ltd
7 Hopetoun Crescent
Edinburgh EH7 4AY

©Chambers Harrap Publishers Ltd 2006

ISBN-13: 978 0550 10301 5
ISBN-10: 0550 10301 5

Author

Daphne Day

Editor

Kate Nicholson

Prepress

Heather Macpherson

Illustrations from Clipart.com

Designed and typeset by Chambers Harrap Publishers Ltd, Edinburgh
Printed and bound:
Hobbs the Printers Ltd, Totton, Hampshire

CHAMBERS HARRAP'S

This resource pack helps you and your class get the most out of **Chambers Harrap's Primary French Dictionary**: there's a page to accompany each scene, followed by 8 pages of photocopiable exercises (solutions on inside front cover). You'll find information to brush up your own French grammar, as well as lots of handy teaching tips and easy activity ideas to save you preparation time. Above all, this pack is designed to help you enjoy teaching French, and your class to enjoy learning it!

BONJOUR LES ENFANTS !

 ## Classroom Language

Bonjour les enfants !
Hello children!

Bonjour les garçons/les filles !
Hello boys/girls!

Au revoir les enfants !
Goodbye children!

Bravo les enfants !
Well done children!

Bravo les verts/les rouges !*
Well done the greens/the reds!

* You can make names for teams using colour adjectives.

 ## Grammar Background

This is for your information – you may not want to make use of it in class.

*The French word for owl is feminine – **la chouette** – this is why the owl says **Je suis votre amie**, using the feminine form of **ami** (friend).*

 ## Using the Dictionary

When a word is underlined in a speech bubble it means you'll find the whole sentence translated if you look up that word.

Get children to guess what a word means before looking it up – they will be keen to find out if they guessed right.

Get the class to look at the sentence **Je vais vous aider à <u>apprendre</u> le français** (page 6) and ask them:

✱ Do we know any of these words?

✱ What do you think the sentence means? (Write a couple of suggestions on the board).

If the class are already competent dictionary users, ask them to look up **apprendre**. If not, show them the entry (<u>page 60</u>).

➲ *See p. 25-26 for photocopiable activities on alphabetical order.*

 ## Language Awareness

Encourage children to spot the differences and similarities between French and English: for example, **enfants** is like *infants*, but there are slight differences in pronunciation, spelling and meaning – *infants* are small children, **enfants** are children of any age.

 ## Language Practice

Pick out children with names similar to French ones, and get the class to pronounce them the French way (with the stress on the last syllable).

➲ *See p. 7 for more information on French names.*

Whole class practice

Teacher	**Bonjour Emma !**
Emma	**Bonjour madame/ monsieur !**
Whole class	**Bonjour Emma !**
Emma	**Bonjour les enfants !**

Group practice

Children take turns to say **Bonjour les enfants !**. Group replies, using the French name or name pronounced in the French way: **Bonjour Matthieu !**, **Bonjour Christine !** etc.

BONJOUR

Grammar Background

When you speak to one child you use a different form of the verb from when you speak to more than one:

Tu vas bien aujourd'hui, Jacques ?

(literally *Are you well today?*, so the answer is **Oui, merci**.)

Vous allez bien aujourd'hui, les enfants ?

When children speak to you they should use the **vous** form:

Vous allez bien aujourd'hui, madame/ monsieur ?

(!) *The verb* **aller** *(to go, to be) is irregular: je vais, tu vas, il/elle va, nous allons, vous allez, ils/elles vont.*

Classroom Language

Écoute, Marianne !
Listen, Marianne!

Écoutez, les enfants !
Listen, children!

Regarde le tableau, Julie !
Look at the board, Julie!

Regardez-moi, les enfants !
Look at me, children!

Dépêche-toi, Marc !
Hurry up, Marc!

Dépêchez-vous, les enfants !
Hurry up, children!

Vas-y, Luc !
Go on, Luc!

Allez-y, les enfants !
Go on, children!

Language Practice

Check that the children say each other's names in a French way.

Pair practice

Catherine	**Tu vas bien aujourd'hui, Christophe ?**
Christophe	**Oui, merci. Et toi Catherine ?**
Catherine	**Moi aussi.**

Whole class practice

The first child you point to asks the second child you point to:

Tu vas bien aujourd'hui, Harry ?

Harry replies and then asks the question to a third child:

Oui, merci. Et toi Anne, tu vas bien aujourd'hui ?

The children can decide who they're going to ask, or you can point to someone.

Using the Dictionary

Look at the picture on <u>page 8</u> and see which words the class can guess the meaning of: **un chat, un chien, une maison** will probably be no problem. **Un toit**, however, might be either be *a tile*, or *a roof*, and **une chambre** may not be obvious at all, except that it's <u>a</u> something. When a problem word emerges, ask for suggested meanings and write them on the board. To speed up dictionary consultation, ask <u>whereabouts</u> in the dictionary the word will be – near the beginning, in the middle or towards the end? (If you haven't got the alphabet on the wall, you may want to write it on the board as a prompt.)

Maison will be in the middle of the dictionary, because it starts with **m**, which is in the middle of the alphabet.

Chambre will be near the beginning, because **c** is near the beginning of the alphabet.

More Classroom Language

Cherchez le mot dans le dictionnaire.
Look up the word in the dictionary.

à la page...
on page...

IL EST L'HEURE DE S'HABILLER

⊃ *See p. 26 for related photocopiable activities on alphabetical order.*

Grammar Background

Masculine and feminine

1. Adjectives ending in **-e** such as **rouge**, **jaune** and **rose** stay the same in the feminine, eg **ma jupe jaune**.

For other adjectives you must add an **e** in the feminine. In the case of **bleu** and **noir** this makes no difference to the pronunciation. In the case of **gris**, **vert**, **lourd** and **prêt** the final consonant is not pronounced in the masculine, but <u>is</u> pronounced in the feminine:

Tu es prêt, Thomas ?
Tu es prê<u>te</u>, Camille ?

J'ai un pull vert.
Elle a une voiture ver<u>te</u>.

Mon pantalon est gris.
Ma chemise est gri<u>se</u>.

Mon cartable est lourd.
La table est lour<u>de</u>.

2. The word for *my* is **mon** with masculine words and **ma** with feminine words:

mon pull bleu / ma robe bleue
mon pantalon jaune / ma chemise jaune

mon jean noir / ma veste noire
mon pyjama blanc / ma jupe blanche

mon tee-shirt rose / ma pantoufle rose
mon anorak vert / ma chaussette verte

* **Mon** is used with feminine words that start with a vowel: **mon amie, mon écharpe**.
* **Mes** is used with all plural words: **mes chaussures noires** (my black shoes), **mes baskets blanches** (my white trainers).

Language Awareness

Un tee-shirt and **un anorak** are the same in English and French. **Un pyjama** and **un jean** are the same except that we don't say <u>a</u> pyjama or <u>a</u> jean in English!

Language Practice

1. De quelle couleur est… ? (*What colour is…?*)

Ask the class about your clothes, adapting these questions to match what you're wearing:

De quelle couleur est ma jupe, noire ou blanche?

De quelle couleur est ma veste, verte ou grise?

De quelle couleur est mon pull, jaune ou rose?

De quelle couleur est mon manteau, rouge ou vert?

De quelle couleur sont mes chaussures, noires ou marron?

(!) *The adjective* **marron** *does not change ending for the feminine or the plural.*

2. French children don't wear school uniform. Get the class to describe theirs.

Write a heading on the board, and get the class to fill the gaps with colour words.

<u>Notre uniforme scolaire</u>
(*Our school uniform*)

un pull _____

une chemise _____

un pantalon _____

une jupe _____ etc

You could also talk about the uniform at another local school, and write the heading **<u>L'uniforme scolaire de…</u>**(*name of school*).

Alternatively, make a poster showing a boy and girl in uniform, and label it.

LE PETIT DÉJEUNER

Grammar Background

When you ask someone if they'd like <u>some</u> bread, <u>some</u> jam or <u>some</u> biscuits, the word for *some* is **du** if the word is masculine, **de la** if it's feminine and **des** if it's plural. If the word starts with a vowel you use **de l'**.

Tu veux...

<u>du</u> pain, <u>du</u> beurre, <u>du</u> sucre, <u>du</u> lait, <u>du</u> miel, <u>du</u> jus, <u>du</u> thé... ?

<u>de la</u> confiture, <u>de la</u> soupe, <u>de la</u> tarte aux pommes... ?

<u>des</u> céréales, <u>des</u> toasts, <u>des</u> œufs... ?

<u>de l'</u>eau ?

⚠ *Note that **céréales** and **toasts** are plural in French.*

Yes please...

When children are speaking to each other they should say **Oui, s'il <u>te</u> plaît** – this is the familiar form. When they speak to a teacher they should say **Oui, s'il <u>vous</u> plaît**.

Using the Dictionary

Ask the class:

Tu veux des <u>grenouilles</u> ? If nobody knows what the word means, tell the class to look it up to see if it's something they'd like to eat. If anyone does know the word, the answer will probably be **NON MERCI**!

Tu veux une <u>souris</u> ? Again, get the children to use the dictionary. At the entry they'll find the phrase **une petite souris, miam, miam**…. This is the opinion of the owl.

➲ *See p. 27 for photocopiable activities on "Oui, s'il vous plaît" and "Non merci".*

Classroom Language

Assieds-toi Pierre, s'il te plaît.
Sit down please, Pierre.

Asseyez-vous les enfants, s'il vous plaît.
Sit down please, children.

Encore une fois s'il te plaît, Louise.
(Do it) one more time please, Louise.

Encore une fois s'il vous plaît, les enfants.
One more time please, children.

Language Practice

Write the following headings and lists on the board.

À boire	À manger
du lait	des céréales
du jus	des toasts
du thé	du pain
du lait chaud	du miel
du laid froid	de la confiture

Practise questions and answers, pointing to the different options to get the **Oui** or **Non** responses:

Tu veux du lait ?
Oui, s'il te plaît.
Non, du jus, s'il te plaît.
Non, du thé, s'il te plaît.

Tu veux des céréales ?
Oui, s'il te plaît.
Non, des toasts, s'il te plaît.
Non, du pain, s'il te plaît.

Tu veux du miel ou de la confiture ?
De la confiture, s'il te plaît.

Tu veux du lait chaud ou du lait froid ?
Du laid froid, s'il te plaît.

EN ROUTE POUR L'ÉCOLE

Grammar Background

The expression **il est l'heure de…** (*it's time to…*) is used with the infinitive (the form of the verb that appears in the dictionary). Some verbs (called <u>reflexive verbs</u>) have **se** as part of their infinitive, eg **se lever** (to get up), **s'asseoir** (to sit down), **s'habiller** (to get dressed). **De** and **se** become **d'** and **s'** before a vowel.

Il est l'heure de <u>s'</u>habiller.
It's time to get dressed.

Il est l'heure d'<u>aller</u> à l'école.
It's time to go to school.

Il est l'heure de <u>déjeuner</u>.
It's time to eat lunch.

Il est l'heure d'<u>aller</u> au lit.
It's time to go to bed.

➲ *Listen to the song "Comment vas-tu y aller ?" on the CD-ROM for more practice with "Il est l'heure de…".*

Language Practice

1. Practise these questions and answers with the children (remember to pronounce their names the French way):

Teacher	**Tu viens, Matthieu ?**
Matthew	**J'arrive, Madame.**
Teacher	**Tu viens, Sarah ?**
Sarah	**J'arrive, Madame.**

2. Draw a clock showing 8 o'clock and label it **Il est l'heure d'aller à l'école.** Practise saying the sentence.

Draw another clock showing the time the French lesson starts, and label it **Il est l'heure <u>de la leçon de français</u>.**

* Do the children recognize the word **leçon**?

* If not, point out that it's very similar to an English word (*lesson*).

Language Awareness

1. If your class are familiar with grammatical terms, ask them which of the words they've been practising are <u>verbs</u> (**Tu <u>viens</u>, J'<u>arrive</u>, <u>aller</u>, <u>apprendre</u>**). If they suggest words which AREN'T verbs, revise nouns, adjectives and verbs.

* A <u>noun</u> is a thing, person, or place, eg bag, mum, France.

* An <u>adjective</u> tells you about a thing, person or place, eg yellow, ready, interesting.

* A <u>verb</u> is a doing word, eg come, go, learn, wait.

The French words they know for clothes, animals and things to eat are <u>nouns</u>. Can they think of some?

The French words they know for colours are <u>adjectives</u>. How many can they remember?

2. Simon says: Put your hand up if you hear a verb!

Teachers are always telling children to <u>do</u> things, so they use a lot of verbs:

<u>Écoutez</u>, les enfants ! (Listen, children!); **<u>Regardez</u>-moi, les enfants !** (Look at me, children!); **<u>Dépêche</u>-toi, Marc !** (Hurry up, Marc!).

Read out the following sentences and tell the class to put their hands up if they hear a verb.

Asseyez-vous, les enfants !

Au revoir, maman.

Bravo Camille !

Merci beaucoup !

J'arrive, Papa.

Écoute-moi, Jacques !

Attendez-moi !

Excusez-moi !

EN CLASSE

Grammar Background

The date is written like this in French: **vendredi 3 mai** (Friday 3 May). To say what the date is, you say **nous sommes le trois mai** (it's the third of May). The names of days of the week and months are NOT written with capitals in French.

The first of the month is **le premier**: **nous sommes le premier mai** (it's the first of May). This is written **1er mai**. To say all the other days of the month you just use the numbers **deux, trois, quatre** etc, so children need to know the numbers up to 31 to talk about dates: **nous sommes le trente novembre** (it's the thirtieth of November).

Language Awareness

Look at the poster on the wall of the classroom (page 16). Which of the words are just like English (**un rectangle, un triangle**)? These words look the same as English, but are pronounced differently in French. **Une figure** looks like English too – but why aren't there any *figures* on the poster? It's because **une figure** in French means a shape, and not a number. Which word is nearly the same as English (**cercle**)? What's different? Is the meaning the same as in English?

Looking at the whole picture, can you find one word which is exactly the same as English, and three words that are nearly the same (**alphabet, classe, mai, toilettes**)?

If anyone suggests **des touches** (keys) you can agree that the word is like *touch*, and keys are something you touch – but you must remember to pronounce the word differently.

Pronunciation

To reinforce the point that words that look the same in French are pronounced differently, make sure that in the French lesson names are pronounced in a French way. Check that the stress goes on the final syllable, eg Char<u>lotte</u>, Da<u>vid</u>, An<u>dré</u>, Amé<u>lie</u>. Children whose names haven't got a French equivalent might like to choose a French one.

Girls' names: Louise, Delphine, Gaëlle, Aurélie, Camille, Aurore, Laurence, Marie, Julie, Charlotte, Lucie, Amélie, Hélène, Léa.

Boys' names: Julien, Pierre, Laurent, Louis, Eric, Thomas, Paul, Nicolas, Hugo, Théo, Clément, Benoît, Florent, Loïc, Matthieu.

Language Practice

Pronounce children's names in an English way and let them correct your pronunciation.

Practise **Mais non !** first, making it very emphatic.

Teacher	**Tu t'appelles David ?**
David	**Mais non ! Je m'appelle Da<u>vid</u>.**
Teacher	**Tu t'appelles Emma ?**
Emma	**Mais non ! Je m'appelle Em<u>ma</u>.**
Teacher	**Tu t'appelles Christopher ?**
Christopher	**Mais non ! Je m'appelle Chris<u>tophe</u>.**
Teacher	**Tu t'appelles Catherine ?**
Catherine	**Mais non ! Je m'appelle Cathe<u>rine</u>.**

FAISONS DES MATHS !

Pronunciation

You don't pronounce the final consonant of **deux** and **trois** when counting, or when they are followed by a consonant, eg **le trois mai**. However, when they are followed by a vowel, for example **deux euros**, **trois ans**, the final consonant is pronounced like **z**. The same applies to **six** and **dix**.

Grammar Background

Saying how old you are

In French you use the verb **avoir** (*to have*) with ages:

Quel âge as-tu ?
How old are you?

J'ai dix ans.
I'm ten (years old).

Thomas a onze ans.
Thomas is eleven (years old).

Note that in French, the number must be followed by the word **ans** (years).

Classroom Language

Faisons un jeu !
Let's have a quiz!

une équipe
a team

Bravo ! C'est la bonne réponse !
Good! That's the right answer!

Désolé ! C'est la mauvaise réponse !
Sorry! That's the wrong answer!

un point
a point

Tu a marqué deux points, Lucie.
You've scored two points, Lucy.

Les rouges ont vingt points.
The reds have twenty points.

Les verts ont vingt-six points.
The greens have twenty-six points.

Les verts ont gagné !
The greens have won!

Language Practice

You can use quizzes to revise any aspect of language. You might want to give extra points for pronunciation – this will help to motivate the children. Keep the score in French.

If children accuse each other of cheating, make them do it in French:

Tu triches !
You're cheating!

Ne triche pas !
Don't cheat!

You could ask questions in English (*What's the French for...?*) or in French – here are some suggestions:

Un cartable, c'est quoi ?
(what is it?)
(a satchel)

C'est une table ou une porte ?
(point to one of two alternatives)
(eg "une porte")

Mon pantalon est de quelle couleur ?
(what colour are my trousers?)
(eg "noir")

C'est combien ?
(point to numbers written on board)
(eg 17: "dix-sept")

Quel jour sommes nous ?
(point to dates written on board)
("nous sommes le...")

You can also practise listening comprehension, giving children points for carrying out the instruction correctly:

Regarde l'ordinateur, Marc !

Regarde mes chaussures, Nicole !

SOURIEZ, S'IL VOUS PLAÎT !

Grammar Background

Giving orders

The verbs Thomas uses as he takes the photos are in the **tu** form: **saute** !; **avance** !; **ris** !. **Souriez, s'il vous plaît !** (*Smile, please!*) is in the **vous** form.

If you want to tell the whole class to do something, you use the **vous** form: **sautez** !; **avancez** !; **riez** !; **reculez** !; **posez les livres** !. This is also the form the children should use to tell <u>you</u> to do things (if you let them!): **sautez, madame** !; **riez, monsieur** !.

Some French imperatives end with **-toi** or **-vous**: **retourne-toi/retournez-vous**; **assieds-toi/asseyez-vous** (literally *turn yourself around*; *sit yourself down*). These imperatives are derived from <u>reflexive verbs</u>. Any verb shown in the dictionary with **se** or **s'** in front of it, such as **se dépêcher** (*to hurry*) or **s'asseoir** (*to sit down*), is reflexive and has either **-toi** or **-vous** on the end of the imperative.

Parts of the body

When you talk about parts of the body in French you generally use **le**, **la** or **les** rather than the equivalent of *my* or *your*: **lève le pied gauche** ! (lift your left foot!); **lève la main, s'il te plaît** ! (put up your hand, please!); **ouvrez les yeux, les enfants** ! (open your eyes, children!).

You only use **ton** or **ta** (*your*) in phrases like **Montre ton oreille** ! and **Touche ton nez** !, where otherwise it would not be clear if it was your ear or nose or someone else's.

Classroom Language

Lève la main, Anne !
Put up your hand, Anne!

Levez la main, les enfants !
Put up your hands, children!

(!) *Note that you use the singular **la main** even when talking to more than one person.*

Essaie, Lara !
Try, Lara!

Essayez, les filles !
Try, girls!

Language Awareness

There are lots of <u>verbs</u> in this scene, and not many <u>nouns</u>.

Do a sorting exercise with the whole class, writing lists like these on the board.

Verbs	Nouns
saute	le <u>pied</u>
touche	ton <u>nez</u>
prends	le <u>livre</u>
retourne-toi	les <u>yeux</u> etc.

Children can do the actions as they do the sorting exercise.

To help with dictionary skills, get the class to put the above lists into alphabetical order. This can be done individually, in pairs or in groups – see how many they can do in 5 minutes.

Language Practice

Pair practice

Children tell each other to do things, using the **tu** form: **Ferme les yeux** !; **Pleure** ! etc.

Whole class practice

Teacher tells the whole class to do things: **pleurez**; **fermez les yeux**; **ouvrez les yeux**; **riez**; **montrez votre nez**; **sautez**; **retournez-vous**; **levez-vous**.

Then pick children to tell <u>you</u> to do things – **Sautez, madame**; **Retournez-vous, monsieur** – but only do what they ask if they use the correct form of the verb.

LE NOUVEAU

 Grammar Background

Masculine and feminine

Nouveau is an <u>adjective</u> meaning *new*; **un nouveau** is *a new boy*. The feminine form of **nouveau** is **nouvelle** – so *a new girl* is **une nouvelle**.

Other adjectives that appear in this scene are **petit**, **grand**, **gros** and **mince**. There is no difference between the pronunciation of **petit** and **petits** in these two phrases:

J'ai un <u>petit</u> frère / Certains sont <u>petits</u> – the final <u>t</u> and <u>ts</u> are not pronounced. But you <u>do</u> pronounce the final <u>t</u> when the word is <u>feminine</u>, eg **J'ai une <u>petite</u> sœur**. The same kind of difference exists between **gros** (no <u>s</u> sound) and **grosse** (<u>s</u> sounded), and **grand** (no <u>d</u> sound) and **grande** (<u>d</u> sounded).

 Language Practice

Do a survey of the whole class, getting children to shout out **moi !** when they fit into a particular category. Write all the categories (**un petit frère** etc) on the board and count up the totals in French.

Qui a un petit frère ?
Who's got a little brother?

Qui a un grand frère ?
Who's got a big brother?

Qui a une petite sœur ?
Who's got a little sister?

Qui a une grande sœur ?
Who's got a big sister?

When you've finished the survey you'll have your headings and totals on the board. Ask the children to compare **un petit frère** and **une petite sœur**, and **un grand frère** and **une grande sœur**.

* What is the difference in spelling?
* Did they notice the different sounds: **petit/petite, grand/grande**?
* What's the reason for the difference?

 Using the Dictionary

Words that change in the feminine

To find out whether an adjective is different in the feminine you can look it up in the dictionary. For example, look up **gros** – what do you find?

The feminine form is **grosse**.

Now look up **mince**. You will see this doesn't change in the feminine.

The children should now be able to complete these sentences:

He is fat.	**Il est _ _ _ _.**
She is fat.	**Elle est _ _ _ _ _ _.**
He is thin.	**Il est _ _ _ _ _.**
She is thin.	**Elle est _ _ _ _ _.**

Words that have more than one meaning: *grand*

How would you describe Max? Is he **petit**? Is he **gros**? Is he **mince**? (He's not small, he's not fat, he is thin). What about **grand**? Yes – but what does **grand** mean? Children will probably think that **grand** = *big*, since they've practised **un grand frère**. If nobody suggests *tall* as a meaning, comment on Max's height – Camille has to look up to him. Could **grand** sometimes mean *tall*? Ask the children to look up **grand** to check.

When everyone has found the word ask how many meanings **grand** has (three : tall, older, large). If children are surprised that *big* isn't there, point out that an <u>older</u> brother is the same as a <u>big</u> brother, and *large* has the same meaning as *big*.

LES MÉTIERS

Grammar Background

In French you don't translate *a* when you say *He's a taxi driver*, or *She's a doctor*: **Il est chauffeur de taxi; Elle est docteur**.

With some jobs the same word is used for men and women; with others there are different masculine and feminine words:

un serveur a waiter
→ **Mon frère est serveur.**
My brother is a waiter.

une serveuse a waitress
→ **Ma sœur est serveuse.**
My sister is a waitress.

un infirmier a (male) nurse
→ **Thomas est infirmier.**
Thomas is a nurse.

une infirmière a (female) nurse
→ **Elle est infirmière.**
She's a nurse.

Other examples are **programmeur/ programmeuse** (programmer), **coiffeur/ coiffeuse** (hairdresser), **avocat/avocate** (lawyer), **policier/femme policier** (police officer).

➲ *See p. 28 for a photocopiable exercise about "Les métiers".*

Classroom Language

Qui sait ?	Who knows?
Personne ?	Nobody?
Je sais.	I know.
Non, je ne sais pas.	No, I don't know.

Language Awareness

Lots of French words are almost the same as English ones. Can the children think of any?

There may be some on the walls of the classroom.

The 20 word challenge!

Tell the children you're going to read a list of 20 French words (see opposite) to see how many of the meanings they can guess. Tell them to put their hands up when they hear a word they don't understand. Write these words on the board under the heading: Words we couldn't guess. The aim is to have as few words on this list as possible.

artiste, acteur, docteur, coiffeur, guitariste, boucher, footballeur, dentiste, architecte, journaliste, fermier, programmeur, mécanicien, pianiste, pilote, professeur, peintre, chef, chauffeur de taxi, électricien.

(!) *The first syllable of **architecte** rhymes with **marsh**, not **mark**.*

The underlined words are those they probably won't recognise. They should know the rest.

Clues

Use these clues to help the children make sense of the unfamiliar words, and encourage them to have <u>no</u> words under the heading <u>Words we couldn't guess</u>.

✳ *Coiffure* is an English word which means *hairdo*. **Se coiffer** in French means *to do your hair*. So what job does a **coiffeur** do? (*hairdresser*)

✳ There is a word in English which starts with *b* and ends with *-cher* (like **boucher**): b_ _ cher. Can you think what it is? It's a type of shopkeeper. (*butcher*)

✳ **Fermier** is like an English word – just take out the **i**, and change one other letter. What do you get? (*farmer*)

✳ If you knock off the last three letters of **mécanicien**, it looks very like an English word. What is it? How do you spell the English word? (*mechanic*)

✳ Listen carefully to **peintre** – it sounds very like an English word that starts with **p**. Nearly all the letters are the same. (*painter*)

✳ In English, a *chauffeur* is someone who drives a rich person's car. So what does a **chauffeur de taxi** do? (*taxi driver*)

11

QUELLE HEURE EST-IL ?

 Language Practice

Listen to the song **Tic, tac** on the CD and get the children to sing it – as many times as they like, so that they master **six heures du matin, huit heures du matin, douze heures/midi, quatre heures de l'après-midi** and **dix heures du soir**.

Pair activity

Write these times on the board: 6a.m., 8a.m., 12a.m., 4p.m., 10p.m..

Pairs practise saying the French for them to each other.

Whole class activity 1

French people use the 24-hour clock when telling the time, instead of saying a.m. and p.m.. Do the children know how it works?

To work out <u>p.m.</u> times by the 24-hour clock, you have to <u>add 12</u> – so **quatre heures de l'après-midi** (4p.m.) is **quatre plus douze** = **seize heures**, which is written 16h.

Put some times on the board and get the class to work out their 24-hour clock:

1p.m.	une heure	=	treize heures 13h
2p.m.	deux heures	=	quatorze heures 14h
3p.m.	trois heures	=	quinze heures 15h
10p.m.	dix heures	=	vingt-deux heures 22h

Whole class activity 2

Write some key times from the school day on the board, and get children to say them. Then fill in what happens at each time. The song has given them the language for going to school, having dinner and going home. You may want to add breaktime (**la récréation**).

Notre journée (*Our day*)

9h   C'est l'heure...................................

(**d'aller à l'école**)

10h   C'est l'heure de.............................

(**la récréation**)

12h   C'est l'heure du.............................

(**déjeuner**)

15h   C'est l'heure...................................

(**d'aller à la maison**)

Bingo

Bingo is a good way of practising numbers and times. Use ready-made cards if you have them. If not, you can practise times as follows.

Divide the class into two teams (or more if you have a big class) such as **les chouettes et les aigles** (the owls and the eagles), and give each team six times to write down:

les chouettes

2p.m. 4a.m. 5p.m. 6a.m. 9p.m. 11a.m.

les aigles

11p.m. 3p.m. 5p.m. 7a.m. 9a.m. 6a.m.

You say the following times, twice each, and the teams cross out their numbers when they hear them. Tell them to shout **bingo !** when all their numbers are crossed out:

cinq heures du soir, dix heures du soir, deux heures de l'après-midi, six heures du matin, midi, trois heures du matin, neuf heures du matin, quatre heures de l'après-midi, sept heures du matin, neuf heures du soir, onze heures du matin, trois heures de l'après-midi, huit heures du soir, une heure de l'après-midi, onze heures du soir.

Bingo ! Les aigles ont gagné !

You can play a similar game with dates, or use more complicated times, such as **huit heures et demi, six heures et quart, six heures moins le quart** etc.

LE MATCH

Grammar Background

When you talk about a sport in French you use the definite article (*the* – **le/la**):

J'aime le tennis.
I like tennis.

Le foot est mon sport favori.
Football is my favourite sport.

When you talk about <u>playing</u> a sport or game you use the verb **jouer** followed by **au**:

Max joue au squash.
Max plays squash.

Camille joue au football.
Camille is playing football.

Au becomes **aux** if the word for the game is plural:

Tu veux jouer aux cartes ?
Do you want to play cards?

Je joue aux jeux électroniques.
I play computer games.

(!) *Chess is a plural word in French* (**les échecs**): **Je joue aux échecs** *(I play chess).*

When you talk about playing a musical instrument, **jouer** is followed by **du** if the instrument is a masculine word:

Paul joue du piano.
Paul plays the piano.

Camille joue du violon.
Camille plays the violin.

If the instrument is feminine, **du** becomes **de la**:

Je joue de la flûte à bec.
I play the recorder.

Mon frère joue de la guitare.
My brother plays the guitar.

Pronunciation

Le football is pronounced almost like in English, but the stress goes on the second syllable instead of the first: **foot<u>ball</u>**. In **le tennis**, the second syllable rhymes with the town **Nice**. In **le ping-pong**, the **i** is pronounced like the **i** in **il**. **Le hockey** is pronounced without an **h**, and the second syllable **'key'** rhymes with *say*.

➲ *See p. 29 for a photocopiable exercise about rhymes.*

Language Practice

The illustrations for **Le match** show that lots of English words are used in the world of sport. **Le football** is also called **le foot** for short. The class can guess what rugby, hockey and golf are in French – yes, **le rugby, le hockey** and **le golf**! **Le cyclisme** (cycling) is a very popular French sport – this word has not been borrowed from English!

Un sondage (*A survey*)

Write the names of the sports you have talked about on the board, like this:

le football	**le golf**
le ping-pong	**le squash**
le tennis	**le rugby**

Ask a few individuals:

Teacher	**Tu joues au football, Henri ?**
Henri	**Oui, madame/monsieur.**
Teacher	**Tu joues au football, Anne ?**
Anne	**Oui, madame/monsieur.**

Then you can ask the whole class: **Qui joue au football ?.**

Get someone to count in French, and write the total under **le football**.

Do the same with the other sports. The answer to **Qui joue au golf?** might be **personne** (nobody), and the total **zéro**.

Finally, declare the result of the survey: **Le sport le plus populaire c'est le_____.**

You could do a similar survey on the musical instruments children play. Then the questions would include **du** (**Qui joue <u>du</u> violon?**) or **de la** (**Tu joues <u>de la</u> flûte à bec?**).

À L'HÔPITAL

Grammar Background

Talking about things that hurt

In French you use the definite article (**le**, **la** or **les**) when talking about parts of the body, rather than the equivalent of *my*: <u>la</u> **jambe**, not <u>ma</u> **jambe**. When the part of the body is masculine (**le pied**), **à** and **le** combine to make **au**: **j'ai mal <u>au</u> pied**. With plural body parts (**les bras**), **à** and **les** combine to make **aux**.

J'ai mal <u>à</u> la jambe.
My leg hurts.

J'ai mal <u>au</u> pied.
My foot hurts.

J'ai mal <u>aux</u> bras.
My arms hurt.

J'ai mal <u>à</u> la tête.
I've got a headache *or* My head hurts.

J'ai mal <u>au</u> ventre.
I've got stomachache.

J'ai mal <u>aux</u> dents.
I've got toothache.

Note that you use the verb **avoir** *(j'ai, tu as, il/elle a, nous avons, vous avez, ils/elles ont)* in these phrases, and when asking someone what's wrong with them:

Qu'est-ce que tu <u>as</u>, David ?
What's wrong with you, David?

Qu'est-ce que vous <u>avez</u>, les garçons ?
What's wrong with you, boys?

Qu'est-ce que tu <u>as</u> à la main ?
What's wrong with your hand?

Qu'est-ce que Thomas <u>a</u> à la jambe ?
What's wrong with Thomas's leg?

Language Practice

Whole class practice

Ask the children what noise they make when something hurts. In French you say **aïe !** (*"aye!"*). See which half of the class can say it with most expression.

Then clutch your head and groan:
Aïe, j'ai mal à la tête !

Get the whole class to repeat it after you a couple of times, and then have half the class say it, then the other, competing to express most pain.

Do the same with other body parts: **Aïe, j'ai mal au ventre/aux dents/au pied** etc.

Pair practice

Explain to the class that **Qu'est-ce que tu as ?** is how you ask what's wrong. Practise it and then have this dialogue with one or two children:

Teacher	**Qu'est-ce que tu as, Emma ?** (Gesturing to head/stomach/ teeth etc)
Emma	**J'ai mal à la tête.**
Teacher	**Pauvre Emma !**

Children can then practise in pairs, taking turns to ask and answer and using all the phrases from the whole class practice.

Game

In the ***Parties du corps*** song on the CD there are phrases you can use to play a version of Simon Says: **Montre ton nez !**; **Touche ton oreille !**; **Tire la langue !** (*Stick out your tongue!*); **Caresse tes cheveux !** (*Stroke your hair!*); **Frotte ton ventre !** (*Rub your tummy!*) etc. (If this is too many verbs for the class, use **Touche** with all the parts of the body.)

Divide the class into teams. Explain that you're going to tell people to do things, but they should only do them if you are polite and say **s'il te plaît**. If you don't, they say **Non !**.

Teacher	**Montre ton nez, Julien !**
Julien	**Non !** *(1 point for his team)*
Teacher	**Montre ton nez, s'il te plaît, Julien !**
Julien	**(points to nose)** *(1 point for his team)*
Teacher	**Tire la langue s'il te plaît, Nicole.**
Nicole	**Non !** *(0 points for her team)*

CACHE-CACHE

Grammar Background

Words like **dans** (*in*), **sur** (*on*), **sous** (*under*), **devant** (*in front of*), **en face de** (*opposite*) and **près de** (*near*) are prepositions. Unlike nouns, adjectives and verbs they always stay the same, but watch out for prepositions with **de**: **de + le → du** and **de + les → des**:

C'est près de l'école.
It's near the school.

C'est près du château.
It's near the castle.

C'est près des toilettes.
It's near the toilets.

When you want to say that something is <u>in</u> a room, cupboard, bag etc you use the preposition **dans** in French.

To talk about being <u>in</u> a country you use **en** when the country is feminine (**en France, en Grande-Bretagne** etc) and **au** when it is masculine (**au Portugal, au Canada** etc).

To talk about being <u>in</u> a town you use **à** (**à Paris, à Londres** etc). This is also used with other types of place, eg **à l'hôpital, à l'école**. It's best to learn such phrases by heart.

Remember that **à + le → au**, and **à + les → aux: au lit** (*in bed*), **aux toilettes** (*in the toilet*).

➲ *See p. 23 for more about countries.*

Language Practice

Talk about where people sit in class using these prepositions: **entre** (*between*), **devant** (*in front of*), **derrière** (*behind*), **en face de** (*opposite*), **a côté de** (*next to*).

Simon est <u>entre</u> Marc et Christophe.

Delphine est <u>devant</u> Jean.

Vrai ou faux ? (*True or false?*)

Teacher	**Marc est entre Simon et Christophe ?**
Class	**Non, c'est faux !**

Teacher	**Christophe est a côté de Simon ?**
Class	**Oui, c'est vrai !**

You can do the same sort of thing with a picture - first discuss where the people or things are, and then make statements about them that are true or false.

Où es-tu ? (*Where are you?*)

Teacher	**Où es-tu, Charlotte ?**
Charlotte	**Je suis en face de Pierre.**
Teacher	**Où es-tu, Jean ?**
Jean	**Je suis derrière Marie.**

C'est qui ? (*Who is it?*)

NB: Don't look at the person you're describing!

Teacher	**Il est devant moi – c'est qui ?**
Class	**C'est Alain !**
Teacher	**Elle est entre Michel et Julie – c'est qui ?**
Class	**C'est Charlotte !**

Children can also do this activity in pairs.

Où est l'ours ? (*Where is the bear?*)

Use a soft toy and a bag or box to demonstrate a variety of prepositions: **l'ours** *(or other toy)* **est sur la table/sur ma tête/sous la chaise/sous mon pull/dans la boîte/derrière Sam/devant le tableau**. You can move the toy around, asking **Où est l'ours maintenant ?**.

Guessing game

Hide a familiar object in the classroom before the lesson. Tell the children this object (eg **l'ours**) is hidden, and get them to guess where it is: **Il est dans le sac ?; Il est dans le tiroir ?; Il est derrière la porte ?; Il est dans le placard ?; Il est sous la table ?**.

(!) *Note that if the object was feminine, you would say **elle** instead of **il**.*

Grammar Background

Speaking politely

Camille politely says **Pardon**. She could have said **Pardon, monsieur**, since it is normal in French to address a stranger as **monsieur** or **madame**. Her response to the **agent de police** should be **Merci, monsieur**. For *You're welcome!* you can say **De rien !**.

The policeman replies to Camille using the polite **vous** form of **prendre** (**prenez** – *take*) because he doesn't know her.

Asking the way

A phrase you often hear when someone tells you the way is **tout droit** (*straight on*). You don't pronounce the t at the end of either word. The adjective **droit** means both *straight* and *right*: **mon bras droit** (*my right arm*); **ma main droite** (*my right hand*).

The expressions **à droite** (*on the right*; *to the right*) and **à gauche** (*on the left*; *to the left*) are also used when giving directions.

(!) *Note that the t IS pronounced in the feminine adjective and noun* **droite**.

Language Practice

Whole class activity: left and right/ putting words into action

For this activity, the class needs to know that **un œil** is used for one eye, while the plural is **les yeux** – do a quick practice if necessary. It doesn't matter if they don't know all the verbs – you can teach them as you go along. They'll know **mettez** by the end of the activity!

Levez la main gauche !
Put up your left hand!

Levez la main droite !
Put up your right hand!

Mettez la main gauche sur la tête !
Put your left hand on your head!

Mettez la main droite sur le ventre !
Put your right hand on your tummy!

Mettez les mains sur la table !
Put your hands on the table!

Mettez les mains sur les yeux !
Put your hands over your eyes!

Mettez la main droite sur la bouche !
Put your right hand over your mouth!

Mettez la main droite sur l'œil droit !
Put your right hand over your right eye!

Mettez la main gauche sur l'œil droit !
Put your left hand over your right eye!

Fermez l'œil droit !
Shut your right eye!

Fermez l'œil gauche !
Shut your left eye!

Regardez à gauche !
Look to the left!

Regardez à droite !
Look to the right!

Language Awareness

Prenez la troisième rue à droite. Prenez la deuxième rue à gauche.

✳ Which streets does the policeman tell Camille to take? If children don't recognize the words **deuxième** and **troisième**, point out that they start with words they know – **deux** and **trois**.

✳ What would **la quatrième rue à droite** be? And **la cinquième**? Can they make some more words like these? (**sixième, septième, huitième, neuvième, dixième**).

(!) *Note that the underlined letters are pronounced z.*

✳ What do you put on the end of English numbers, which is like **-ième** in French? (**-th**, eg fourth).

✳ In English you don't put -**th** on the end of one, two or three. What about French – are there any numbers you can't add -**ième** to?

➲ *Look at page 95 of the dictionary to find out.*

AU SUPERMARCHÉ

Grammar Background

Definite or indefinite?

When you talk about your likes and dislikes in French you always use the definite article, **le**, **la** or **les** – that's why Max says **J'adore la glace**.

Tu aimes les fraises ?
Do you like strawberries?

Oui, j'aime tous les fruits.
Yes, I like all fruit.

Je n'aime pas le fromage.
I don't like cheese.

Je n'aime pas les tomates.
I don't like tomatoes.

(!) *Note that in French, **un fruit** = a piece of fruit; **les fruits** = fruit in general.*

When you're asking for something, or offering something, you use **un** or **une**, or the words that mean *some* (**de la**, **du**, **des**):

Tu veux une banane ?
Do you want a banana?

Tu veux un fruit ?
Do you want a piece of fruit?

Je veux de la pastèque.
I want some water melon.

Je veux du fromage.
I want some cheese.

Je veux des petits pois.
I want some peas.

N'oublie pas la glace !

To tell someone **not** to do something you use **ne** (or **n'** in front of a vowel) and **pas** on either side of the verb.

Ne bouge pas ! / Ne bougez pas !
Don't move!

N'oublie pas de faire tes devoirs ! / N'oubliez pas de faire vos devoirs!
Don't forget to do your homework!

(!) *If you're using **vous** the verb will usually end with -ez. Two notable exceptions are **dites !** (say) and **faites !** (do!).*

Language Practice

Whole class activity: preferences

Ask children which fruit or vegetable they prefer:

Qu'est-ce que tu préfères, Julien, les pommes ou les poires ?

Qu'est-ce que tu préfères, Anne, les carottes ou les tomates ?

Children reply **Les...** in each case. (If anyone hates both they can say **Je n'aime pas les carottes et je n'aime pas les tomates.**)

Pair activity

It's important to get your healthy 5-a-day-fruit and vegetables, even when you're in France! Get the pairs to make a shopping list in French of 5 fruits and vegetables they both like, then choose one person to read it out to the class.

Whole class activity: the top five

Give each child a picture of a different fruit or vegetable and a name to go with it: **Matthieu, tu es Monsieur Carottes; Marie, tu es Madame Pommes** etc.

Then get the pairs to read out the lists they made earlier, eg **les bananes, les pommes de terre, les tomates, les pommes, les fraises**. All the children whose fruit or vegetable appears on the list gets a point, so **Monsieur Bananes, Madame Pommes de terre** etc mark 1 on their scoresheets.

When all the pairs have read out their lists, see which fruits and vegetables are the most popular: **Monsieur Bananes, tu as combien de points?** etc. Write the most popular items on the board under the headings **1er, 2ème, 3ème, 4ème, 5ème**.

AU RESTAURANT

Grammar Background

Avoir...

In French you use the verb **avoir** to say that you're hungry or thirsty, and hot or cold:

Tu as soif ?
Are you thirsty?

J'ai très soif.
I'm very thirsty.

Tu as faim ?
Are you hungry?

Non, je n'ai pas faim.
No, I'm not hungry.

J'ai froid.
I'm cold.

J'ai chaud.
I'm hot.

Asking questions

When you ask a question in English you usually put the verb first, eg *Can I help you?* In a statement the verb does not come first, eg *I can help you*.

You can put the verb first in French questions too: **Parlez-vous français ?**.

Alternatively, you can just make a statement in a questioning tone of voice: **Vous parlez français ?**. This is common in spoken language, and is how the waiter and Thomas ask questions in this scene:

La soupe est pour vous ?
Is the soup for you?

Je peux avoir un autre jus d'orange ?
Can I have another orange juice?

In English, question words such as *what, who* and *when* nearly always come at the beginning of the question, eg *What colour is it?*; *When does it start?*.

In French questions, the expression **qu'est-ce que** (*what?*) always comes first:

Qu'est-ce que vous voulez manger ?
What do you want to eat?

Qu'est-ce que c'est ?
What is it?

But other question words can come at the start or the end of the sentence:

Où est-elle ? / Elle est où ?
Where is she?

Quand arrives-tu ? / Tu arrives quand ?
When are you arriving?

In French you can also start a question by mentioning the thing you're going to ask about:

La soupe, c'est pour qui ?
Who's the soup for?

You may find that this type of question works better in the classroom, since it gives a clear signal what the question is going to be about:

Un avocat, c'est quoi ?
What is 'un avocat'?

Cette fille, c'est qui ?
Who's that girl?

Un jus d'orange, c'est combien ?
How much is an orange juice?

Language Practice

Game: C'est qui? (*Who is it?*)

Can the class guess who you're thinking about? (Be careful not to look at the person!).

They can ask questions about the person's clothes, where they're sitting, their hobbies etc.

If you tell them the person is a girl they can ask questions like:
Elle a un pull bleu ?; **Elle est grande ?**; **Elle est petite ?**; **Elle est mince ?**; **Elle joue du piano ?**; **Elle est en face de Pierre ?**; **Elle est toujours en retard ?**; **Elle a un cartable noir ?**; **Elle s'appelle Léa ?** etc.

If you tell them it's a boy they can ask:
Il est petit ?; **Il est grand ?**; **Il est derrière Chantal ?**; **Il joue au football ?**; **Il n'aime pas les fruits ?** etc.

You could also ask a child to think of a person, and to answer the questions from the class. Get them to whisper the name to you first so you can help if necessary.

TEMPS LIBRE

➲ *See p. 32 for a photocopiable activity relating to this topic.*

Grammar Background

Look at this dialogue on <u>page 27</u>:

Camille	**Quel jour tu préfères ?**
	(literally: *Which day do you prefer?*)
Thomas	**Le dimanche.**
Camille	**Pourquoi ?**
Thomas	**Parce que le dimanche je ne vais pas à l'école.**

➲ *See p. 31 for a photocopiable activity on "pourquoi" and "parce que".*

Note that **le dimanche** means both *Sunday* and *on Sundays.*

Thomas has a negative reason for liking Sundays: **Je ne vais pas**.... To make negative sentences you put **ne** (or **n'** before a vowel) and **pas** on either side of the verb.

The class may have positive reasons for liking a particular day:

Le dimanche je vais à la piscine.
On Sundays I go to the swimming pool.

Le samedi je vais en ville.
On Saturdays I go into town.

Le samedi je peux faire ce que je veux.
On Saturdays I can do what I like.

Le weekend je joue avec mes amis.
At weekends I play with my friends.

Language Practice

Quel jour tu préfères?

Revise the days of the week – the class could recite them in chorus. Then ask a few children **Quel jour tu préfères ?**. If the first three or four all say **Le samedi**, ask **Tout le monde préfère le samedi ?** (*Does everyone like Saturday best?*).

If there are other favourites write **le samedi, le dimanche** etc on the board, and see how many votes each day gets.

⚠ *Remember that the days of the week do not have capital letters in French.*

Sentence building – remembering how words fit together

1. Pourquoi tu préfères le samedi ?
→ **Parce que je ne vais pas à l'école.**

You can teach this as the answer and practise it. Then write it on the board with one word missing: **Parce que je ne ____ pas à l'école.** Get the class to read it out, adding the missing word. Then rub out another word: **Parce que je ne ____ pas à _____.** Keep going until there are only lines on the board to show where the words should be, and the class are chanting the whole sentence from memory.

2. Pourquoi tu préfères le samedi ?
→ **Parce que le samedi je peux faire ce que je veux.**

This answer may look too complicated for your class, but they know all the words, and the words are easy to say (**que, peux** and **veux** all rhyme). The only problem is stringing them together in the right order. If you emphasize the rhyming words during the rubbing out process the sentence will be more memorable.

Variation

Make a set of cards each bearing one word from the sentence, ie **parce, que, le, samedi, je, peux, faire, ce, veux.** Give each child a word (so two or three will have **parce**, two or three will have **que** etc). When you point to the words in the sentence, the children with **parce** shout their word, and so on. The children who've got **que** and **je** get two goes. After a few practices, rub out the sentence and see if they can still do it. If they have mastered it you can swap the cards around and have another go.

AU CIRQUE

Grammar Background

Plurals

With most French nouns, an **s** is added to form the plural, eg **une fille, deux filles**. With other nouns, such as those ending in **-eau** or **-eu**, an **x** is added instead, eg **un manteau, deux manteaux; un jeu, deux jeux**. Note that neither the **s** nor the **x** is pronounced.

The words **animal**, **journal** (*newspaper*) and **cheval** (*horse*) are different: the **-al** of the singular changes to **-aux** in the plural: **Je veux voir les animaux** (*I want to see the animals*). The **x** is still not pronounced, but the plural word <u>does</u> sound different from the singular. The plural of the word for *a pet* – **un animal de compagnie** – is **des animaux de compagnie**.

Pronouns

The word **les** means both *the* and *them*:

Tu n'aimes pas <u>les</u> clowns ? Si, je <u>les</u> adore.
Don't you like clowns? Yes, I love them.

When **les** means *them* it goes in front of the verb, eg **Je les connais** (*I know them*), **Je les vois** (*I can see them*). The only exception to this is when the verb is an imperative: **Regardez-les !** (*Look at them!*)

The word **le** means both *the* and *him*:

Tu vois Marc ? Oui, je <u>le</u> vois.
(*Can you see Marc? Yes, I can see him.*)

The word **la** means both *the* and *her*:

Tu vois Nicole ? Oui, je <u>la</u> vois.
(*Can you see Nicole? Yes, I can see her.*)

Language Practice

Whole class practice

The class need to know the phrases **je le connais; je la connais; je les connais** (*I know him; I know her; I know them*) for these exercises.

Teacher	**Tu connais Max, Charlotte ?**
Charlotte	**Oui, je le connais.**

Teacher	**Tu connais Charlotte, Max ?**
Max	**Oui, je la connais.**
Teacher	**Tu connais Charlotte et Max, André ?**
André	**Oui, je les connais.**

When the class has mastered the pronouns, change the pattern, so that the person who answers chooses who to ask next:

Teacher	**Tu connais Marie, Charlotte ?**
Charlotte	**Oui, je la connais. Tu connais Paul, Delphine ?**
Delphine	**Oui, je le connais. Tu connais Claire et Marc, Robert ?**
Robert	**Oui, je les connais.**

Using "si"

Si is used instead of **oui** when you want to answer "yes" to a negative question.

Demonstrate this usage, making your answers very emphatic:

Tu n'aimes pas Marie ?
→ Si, je l'adore !

Tu n'aimes pas Claire et Marc ?
→ Si, je les adore !

You can ask the class questions like this or, if they're not keen on declaring their love for each other, use **Tu ne connais pas…** and **Si, je le/la/les connais** instead.

More difficult variation

Tu vois…? The answer to this may be *yes* or *no* (tell the children not to look around).

If the answer is *no*, children need to add **ne** and **pas** to the sentence, putting **ne** in front of **le, la** or **les**: **je ne le vois pas; je ne la vois pas; je ne les vois pas**:

Teacher	**Tu vois Max, Chantal ?**
Chantal	**Oui, je le vois.**
Teacher	**Tu vois Chantal, Max ?**
Max	**Non, je ne la vois pas.**

LA TEMPÊTE

Grammar Background

Les saisons

le printemps	the spring
→ **au printemps**	in the spring
l'été	the summer
→ **en été**	in the summer
l'automne	the autumn
→ **en automne**	in the autumn
l'hiver	the winter
→ **en hiver**	in the winter

la saison de football
the football season

Quelle saison...?
Which season...?

⚠ *Note that the names of months and seasons do not have capital letters in French.*

Language Awareness

Which words in the scenes are similar to English ones? (**les saisons**, **l'automne**). The word **la tempête** is like the English word *tempest* – do the class know what it means? Some are not so obvious: **le <u>soleil</u>** starts like the English word *solar* – a solar eclipse is an eclipse of the sun, a solar panel collects heat from the sun. **La <u>lune</u>** starts like the word *lunar* – a lunar landing is a landing on the moon.

What about **un éclair**? What does it mean in the picture? What's an *éclair* in English?

In fact, **un éclair** can be two things in French: either a flash of lightning, or a delicious **éclair au chocolat**.

Syllables

Are the French words longer or shorter than the English words? Is there any difference in length between **les saisons** and *the seasons*? What about **automne** and *autumn*? **Automne** has one more letter – but does it take any longer to say the French word than the English word? No, because the two words have the same number of <u>syllables</u> (two).

If the class is not familiar with the term, demonstrate how words can be divided up: com-pu-ter; un-ne-ces-sa-ry; sci-en-ti-fi-cal-ly. Get them to write their names divided up into syllables, working in pairs so they can help each other. Have some of them read out their names: Ni-co-la Ro-bin-son etc. See who has the most syllables in their first name. How many people's names have only one syllable? (eg Paul, Kate, Mark, Luke, Claire, Jack).

Then give them half a dozen words they've learned recently to divide up, for example **banane**, **concombre**, **tomate**, **carotte**, **fraise**, **melon**, **avocat** (ba-nane, con-combre, to-mate, ca-rotte, fraise, me-lon, a-vo-cat).

➲ *See p. 31 for a photocopiable exercise on counting syllables.*

Language Practice

Whole class practice

Revise the months of the year by asking what season they are:

Janvier, c'est l'hiver ?
Oui.

Avril, c'est l'hiver ?
Non, c'est le printemps.

Pair work

Get the children to ask each other about the seasons and months of their birthdays:

Ton anniversaire, c'est en hiver ?
(Is it in the winter?) → **Non.**

Ton anniversaire, c'est au printemps ?
(Is it in the spring?) → **Oui.**

En avril ? → **Non.**

En mai ? → **Oui.**

Then ask them to report back to the class:

Teacher	**L'anniversaire de Luc, c'est quand, David ?**
David	**C'est au printemps, en mai.**

LA NATURE

Grammar Background

The phrase **il y a** means there is/there are.

Language Practice

Tu as une bonne mémoire ?

Tell the class they're going to draw a picture – the one on <u>page 47</u> of the dictionary. Give them three minutes to look at it and listen to you saying the words. They should repeat the words after you to help them remember the details. When the three minutes are up they can start drawing (it doesn't have to be detailed). Describe the picture to jog their memories (note that the <u>d</u> of **nid** and the <u>c</u> of **tronc** are not pronounced):

Il y a un arbre ; <u>dans</u> l'arbre il y a un <u>nid</u>.

<u>Dans</u> le nid il y a <u>trois petits oiseaux</u>.

Il y a un <u>gros oiseau</u> qui leur donne à manger.

<u>Dans</u> l'arbre il y a aussi <u>la chouette</u>.

<u>Sous</u> l'arbre il y a une <u>tente</u>.

<u>Sous</u> le nid <u>à droite</u> il y a une <u>araignée</u>.

<u>À côté de</u> l'arbre il y a <u>un garçon et une fille</u>.

<u>Devant</u> le garçon et la fille il y a <u>une grenouille</u>.

<u>À droite</u> il y a <u>un homme et une femme</u>.

Alternatively, if you think the class would find so much French over-whelming, you could do it like this:

N'oubliez pas l'arbre.
Don't forget the tree.

N'oubliez pas la chouette.
Don't forget the owl.

When they've finished their drawings, let them look at the picture, and go over the words again, checking who remembered each detail:

Qui a l'arbre ?
Who's got the tree?

Qui a la tente ?
Who's got the tent?

Bravo to anyone who remembered **la plume**, **les feuilles**, or **la route**!

La géographie

Ask children which geographical words in the "Géographie" insert on <u>page 46</u> they recognize. Then put these categories on the board and see if the class can give you an example of each:

un continent - un désert - une île – une mer - un océan - une jungle - un volcan

Then ask the whole class questions to help you correctly fill in each category:

Le Pacifique, c'est une mer ou un océan ?

L'Etna, c'est un volcan ou une île ?

Le Sahara, c'est une jungle ou un désert ?

Some suggestions...

continents:	**l'Amérique, l'Afrique, l'Europe**
deserts:	**le Gobi, le Kalahari**
islands:	**Tenerife, la Crète**
seas:	**la Méditerranée**
oceans:	**l'Atlantique, l'Arctique**
jungles:	**l'Amazonie**
volcanoes:	**le Vésuve, le Krakatoa**

If the class don't recognize a word, help them spot similarities to the English.

LES VACANCES

Grammar Background

Où vas-tu ? (*Where are you going?*)

✳ **Je vais à…**

When you're talking about going <u>to a place</u> the word for *to* is **à**:

Je vais à la mer/à Blackpool/à Paris.
I'm going to the seaside/to Blackpool/to Paris.

(!) *Note that when the place has a masculine name (eg **le Portugal**), à + le → **au**:*

Nous allons au Portugal/au Pays de Galles.
We're going to Portugal/to Wales.

Tu veux aller au cinéma ?
Do you want to go to the cinema?

(!) *Note that when the place has a plural name (eg **les États-Unis**), à + les → **aux**:*

Nous allons aux États-Unis.
We're going to the United States.

Je vais aux toilettes.
I'm going to the toilet.

✳ **Je vais en…**

When the place you're going to is a <u>continent</u>, eg **l'Australie**, a <u>feminine country</u>, eg **la France** or **l'Écosse** (most countries are feminine), or a <u>feminine state</u>, eg **la Floride**, the word for *to* is **en**:

Je vais en Australie/en Europe.
I'm going to Australia/to Europe.

Je vais en France/en Inde/en Floride.
I'm going to France/to India/to Florida.

Although **à** is used with the names of towns and cities, the phrase *I'm going into town* is translated as **je vais <u>en</u> ville**.

✳ **Je vais chez…**

When the place you're going to is someone's <u>house</u>, <u>shop</u> or <u>workplace</u>, the word for *to* is **chez**:

Je vais chez mes grands-parents.
I'm going to my grandparents' house.

Je vais chez le marchand de journaux.
I'm going to the paper shop.

Je vais chez le dentiste.
I'm going to the dentist.

If you're not going anywhere you also use **à**, **en** and **chez**, because these words can also mean *at* and *in*:

Nous restons à Londres.
We're staying in London.

Tu restes en Écosse ?
Are you staying in Scotland?

Je reste chez moi.
I'm staying at home.

Qu'est-ce que tu vas faire ? (*What are you going to do?*)

Je vais jouer avec mes amis.
I'm going to play with my friends.

Je vais faire du vélo.
I'm going to ride my bike.

Je vais faire du camping.
I'm going to go camping.

Je vais faire du ski.
I'm going to go skiing.

Language Practice

Tes vacances de rêves (*Your dream holiday*)

Ask for (or teach) some names of continents, countries and activities, write them on the board and have a vote to find which are the most popular. Alternatively, pairs can work together to choose.

Continent	Pays	Activité
l'Australie	la France	le camping
l'Europe	le Portugal	le vélo
l'Amérique	l'Écosse	la plage
l'Afrique	l'Espagne	le ski

LA FÊTE

Grammar Background

The words **son**, **sa** and **ses** mean both *his* and *her*. You use the masculine adjective **son** with masculine nouns, such as **ami**, **père** and **cartable**, and the feminine **sa** with feminine words like **amie**, **mère** and **voiture**:

Louis et son père/sa mère
Louis and his father/his mother

Élodie et son père/sa mère
Élodie and her father/her mother

You use the plural adjective **ses** with plural nouns:

Camille et ses amies
Camille and her (female) friends

Max et ses amis
Max and his friends

To say *Thomas's friends* in French, you literally say *the friends of Thomas*: **les amis de Thomas**.

l'anniversaire de Thomas
Thomas's birthday
→ **son anniversaire**
his birthday

la fête de Thomas
Thomas's party
→ **sa fête**
his party

les cadeaux de Thomas
Thomas's presents
→ **ses cadeaux**
his presents

Language Practice

Whole class practice: C'est mon anniversaire (*It's my birthday*)

Find out if it's anyone's birthday today, or if anyone has one coming up.

Teacher	**Aujourd'hui, c'est l'anniversaire de quelqu'un ?**
Child	**Oui, c'est mon anniversaire.**
Teacher	**Demain, c'est l'anniversaire de quelqu'un ?**
Child	**Oui, c'est mon anniversaire demain.**
Teacher	**Samedi, c'est l'anniversaire de quelqu'un ?** etc

Alternatively, if you have a birthday list for your class you can ask about dates that will interest them:

Le premier mai, c'est l'anniversaire de quelqu'un ?

Le quatre juillet, c'est l'anniversaire de quelqu'un ?

To make it easier, point to dates on the calendar when asking the questions.

Pair practice: other people's birthdays

Pairs ask each other **Ton anniversaire, c'est quand ?** and make a note of the answer, writing down the date in the French way. You then prompt each person to tell the class about their partner: **L'anniversaire de Max, c'est le cinq avril.**

Homework

Write a French invitation to your next birthday party. You may need to change **dixième** to another word like **neuvième** or **onzième**. Look at <u>page 95</u> of the dictionary for more words like this.

Who are you going to invite? Here are some possibilities: **ma mère, mon père, mon cousin, ma cousine, ma grand-mère, mon grand-père, mon frère, ma sœur, ma tante, mon oncle, mon ami, mon amie**. Make **une liste d'invités** (guest list).

ALPHABETICAL ORDER 1

a b c d e f g h i j k l m n o p q r s t u v w x y z

EXERCISE 1

Henri is a young wizard who's learning spells at school. He knows the spell that turns dragons into kittens is something like **janvier septembre octobre novembre**. But the dragon is getting closer and closer, and the spell isn't working! "Try alphabetical order!" suggests his friend Pénélope.

1 _____ 2 _____ 3 _____ 4 _____

Phew! Just in time.
There's another spell for snakes, something like **mars janvier avril novembre**. Can you put those words in the right order for Henri?

1 _____ 2 _____ 3 _____ 4 _____

Henri is sure he's got the the rolling rock spell right: **avril juin janvier mai** – but he hasn't! Can you make it right?

1 _____ 2 _____ 3 _____ 4 _____

[When there are words starting with the same letter in a list, such as John, Jane and Jill, you have to look at the <u>second</u> letter to put them in order: J<u>a</u>ne, J<u>i</u>ll, J<u>o</u>hn.]

This time the whole school is shaking because a giant is hammering on the door. Henri knows the words in the spell to fix giants are **avril juin mars mai**, so why is the giant still there? Quick, help him correct the alphabetical order!

1 _____ 2 _____ 3 _____ 4 _____

[When there are words starting with the same two letters in a list, such as Jane, Jack and Jaqueline, you have to look at the <u>third</u> letter to put them in order: Ja<u>c</u>k, Ja<u>n</u>e, Ja<u>q</u>ueline.]

EXERCISE 2

> ### Riddle: When does Friday come before Thursday?
> ### When it's in alphabetical order!

This is the order we usually put the days of the week in: Monday, Tuesday, Wednesday, Thursday, Friday, Saturday, Sunday. Can you put them in <u>alphabetical</u> order?

1 _____ 2 _____ 3 _____ 4 _____

5 _____ 6 _____ 7 _____

Now see if you can complete this riddle:

> ### When is _____ the last day of the week?
> ### When it's in alphabetical order!

ALPHABETICAL ORDER 2

a b c d e f g h i j k l m n o p q r s t u v w x y z

EXERCISE 1

Camille is never ready on time – she can never find anything because her room is such a mess. Maybe if her wardrobe was in alphabetical order it would help. Can you sort her clothes out? There's a **skirt**, an **anorak**, **trousers**, a **dress**, a **coat** and a **jacket**.

1 _____ 2 _____ 3 _____ 4 _____ 5 _____ 6 _____

Now can you write the French words for these clothes?

1 _____ 2 _____ 3 _____ 4 _____ 5 _____ 6 _____

That's spoilt her nice tidy alphabetical order – can you sort it out for her again?

1 _____ 2 _____ 3 _____ 4 _____ 5 _____ 6 _____

EXERCISE 2

What colour are the clothes?

You can find out by putting these colours into alphabetical order.

rose, verte, bleu, rouge

1 _____ 2 _____ 3 _____ 4 _____

Now put colour number one in sentence 1, and so on.

1 Le pull est _____.   2 La robe est _____.

3 Le manteau est _____.   4 La veste est _____.

Can you find what these colours are called in English?

1 _____ 2 _____ 3 _____ 4 _____

Are they still in alphabetical order? Can you sort them out?

1 _____ 2 _____ 3 _____ 4 _____

EXERCISE 3

Can you complete the words to make the alphabet? There is only one word beginning with **k** in the dictionary – can you find it and put it in the gap?

a _ _ (friend)   **b** _ _ _ _ _ _ (hello)   **c** _ _ _ _ (dog)   **d** _ _ _ (sheet)

e _ _ _ _ _ _ (children)   **f** _ _ _ _ (girl)   **g** _ _ _ _ _ (boy)   **h** _ _ _ _ (time)

i _ (he)   **j** _ _ _ (skirt)   **k** _ _ _ _ _ _   **l** _ _ _ _ _ (washbasin)

m _ _ _ (mother)   **n** _ _ _ (black)   **o** _ _ _ (bear)   **p** _ _ _ (father)

q _ _ _ _ _ _ _ (question)   **r** _ _ _ (dress)   **s** _ _ _ _ (soap)   **t** _ _ _ _ _ _ _ (t-shirt)

26   **u** _ (one)   **v** _ _ _ _ (jacket)   **w**   **x**   **y** _ _ _ _ _ (yoghurt)   **z**

USING THE DICTIONARY

EXERCISE 1

Oui, s'il vous plaît or *Non merci*?

Thomas and his cat Minou don't always like the same things to eat and drink. For each item in the list opposite, write **oui** if you think Thomas or Minou <u>would</u> like it, and **non** if they <u>wouldn't</u>. Look up any words you don't know in the dictionary.

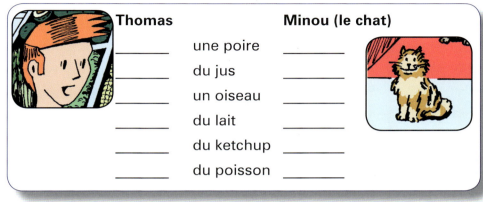

Thomas		Minou (le chat)
_____	une poire	_____
_____	du jus	_____
_____	un oiseau	_____
_____	du lait	_____
_____	du ketchup	_____
_____	du poisson	_____

Now answer these questions with **Oui, s'il vous plaît** or **Non merci**:

Tu veux du jus, Thomas ?   _____

Tu veux une poire, Minou ?_____

EXERCISE 2

Luc is a vegetarian. Tick the things he will eat from this list.

du porc	une banane	des pâtes	des pommes de terre
des tomates	des cerises	du jambon	des céréales
des fraises	des saucisses	des avocats	du miel

Charlotte is on a strange diet – she only eats red things!

What are the three things she will eat from the list above?

_____   _____   _____

EXERCISE 3

Danger ! Requins !

Should you run away, call the police, hide, or what?

Do you know the meaning of **requins**? If not, quick – look it up in the dictionary before it's too late, and tick the right warning.

☐ Don't light a fire here.

☐ Don't swim here.

☐ Don't touch anything here.

EXERCISE 4

Congratulations! You've won a French raffle.
You can choose one of these prizes:

une montre ↙

une voiture

un vélo

Use the dictionary if you're not sure what the prizes are. Then write your choice in the gap.

Je veux _____ s'il vous plaît.

NOUS SOMMES EN RETARD !

We're late!

Thierry, Charlotte, Max, Marie, Nicole and Luc are all late for work.

Do you know what their jobs are? Use your dictionary if you don't know all the words.

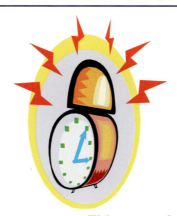

Thierry est fermier.	He's a _____.
Charlotte est chirurgien.	She's a _____.
Max est coiffeur.	He's a _____.
Marie est chauffeur de taxi.	She's a _____.
Nicole est gardien de but.	She's a _____.
Luc est programmeur.	He's a _____.

They're all late because they can't find one vital thing they need to do their job.

Can you work out who would use each of the items below, and write their name in the gap?

Voilà tes clés, _____

Voilà ton masque, _____

Voilà ton ballon, _____

Voilà tes ciseaux, _____

Voilà ta souris, _____

Voilà ton chien, _____

WORDS THAT RHYME

EXERCISE 1

Does your name rhyme with any other word?

The name *Mark* rhymes with lots of words – can you think of some?

____

What about *Penelope* – does that rhyme with anything?

Estelle and **Aurore** are French names that rhyme with other words:

Je m'appelle Estelle.

J'adore Aurore.

EXERCISE 2

C'est qui? (*Who is it?*)

Can you find the name that rhymes with the word in the question? Write it in the gap.

Qui est au **lit** ? __________ Max / Camille / Estelle

Qui est dans la salle de **bains** ? __________ Luc / Marie / Alain

Qui est à la **mer** ? __________ Pierre / Martin / Mohammed

Qui est à l'**école** ? __________ Alexia / Nicole / Christophe

Qui est à la **piscine** ? __________ Fatima / Mehdi / Delphine

EXERCISE 3

Odd one out

Three of the **bold** words (or bits of words) in the boxes rhyme, and one doesn't. Cross out the one that doesn't.

Quelle **heure** est-il ?
Léa est ma **sœur**.
C'est **pour** toi.
Ma mère est profes**seur**.

Mon pull est **gris**.
Je vais au **lit**.
Bonjour, Jul**ie**.
Ma jupe est **grise**.

Vous voulez du **vin** ?
Lève la **main**.
J'ai très **faim**.
Tu **vas** bien, aujourd'hui ?

Mon pantalon est **vert**.
Ma chemise est **verte**.
Tu veux un **verre** d'eau ?
Où est ton **père** ?

THE SAME BUT DIFFERENT...

EXERCISE 1

Danger, poison, clown, page, triangle, art, football...

Lots of words look the same in French and English, and mean the same thing. But some words can trick you: they <u>look</u> the same, but they <u>mean</u> something different. For example, **un car** means *a bus* in French.

Here are some tricky words – can you find the right words in the box to complete the sentences?

French   **English**

grapes, shape, jacket, sport, colour, number, for colouring, flower, container, for writing, underwear, dried fruit

Le basket is a _____.   A basket is a _____.

Une figure is a _____.   A figure is a _____.

Une veste is a _____.   A vest is _____.

Rose is a _____.   A rose is a _____.

Un crayon is _____.   A crayon is _____.

Du raisin means _____.   Raisins are _____.

EXERCISE 2

Some lookalike words <u>mean</u> the same thing, but are <u>spelled</u> differently: for example, **dictionnaire** has two **n**'s, and a different ending from *dictionary.*

Write the English for these French words, without looking in the dictionary.

French	English	French	English
mon adresse	_____	une girafe	_____
une carotte	_____	une enveloppe	_____
novembre	_____	un journaliste	_____
une guitare	_____	un squelette	_____
une raquette	_____	un yaourt	_____

Now check your English spelling by looking up the French words in the dictionary.

What was your score out of 10?

_____

10/10 Excellent !
9/10 Très bien !
8/10 Bien !
7/10 Assez bien !
Moins de 6/10 Hmm...

POURQUOI TU FAIS ÇA ?

Why are you doing that?

Here are some silly answers about why people are doing things.
Can you match up the real answer to each question?

1 Pourquoi tu manges un sandwich ?

2 Pourquoi tu ris ?

3 Pourquoi tu bois un jus d'orange ?

4 Pourquoi tu pleures ?

5 Pourquoi tu portes un manteau ?

6 Pourquoi tu ouvres la fenêtre ?

7 Pourquoi tu vas à la piscine ?

8 Pourquoi tu vas vite ?

9 Pourquoi tu ne viens pas ?

10 Pourquoi tu ne vas pas à l'école ?

A Parce que c'est samedi.

B Parce qu'il fait froid.

C Parce que je suis en retard.

D Parce que c'est drôle.

E Parce que je veux nager.

F Parce que je ne veux pas.

G Parce que j'ai très, très faim.

H Parce que je suis triste.

I Parce que j'ai soif.

J Parce qu'il fait trop chaud.

SYL-LA-BLE SA-FA-RI PARK

Syl-la-ble Sa-fa-ri Park is an interesting place – all the animals are French, and it has three enclosures: Area One is for animals with one-syllable names, Area Two is for animals with two-syllable names and Area Three is for all the others. Can you put these new arrivals in the right Area?

Area One	Area Two	Area Three

une girafe
un hippopotame
un éléphant
un ours
un lion
un zèbre
un crocodile
un pingouin
un tigre
un kangourou
un gorille

À MON AVIS...

In my opinion...

Here are 12 ways of spending your time. Are they good things to do?
Tick the opinion you agree with most.

Use the dictionary if you don't understand a word.

> **! C'est mieux que... = *It's better than...***

apprendre le français,...
- ☐ c'est amusant
- ☐ c'est difficile mais amusant
- ☐ c'est amusant et facile
- ☐ c'est impossible

jouer au golf,...
- ☐ c'est amusant
- ☐ c'est super
- ☐ c'est très difficile
- ☐ ce n'est pas très amusant

aller à l'école,...
- ☐ c'est intéressant
- ☐ ce n'est pas très amusant
- ☐ c'est mieux que de nager avec des requins
- ☐ c'est intéressant et amusant

manger une glace,...
- ☐ c'est difficile
- ☐ c'est agréable
- ☐ c'est amusant
- ☐ c'est dangereux

jouer aux jeux vidéo,...
- ☐ c'est intéressant
- ☐ c'est mieux que de jouer au football
- ☐ c'est mieux que de faire des maths
- ☐ c'est difficile

nager,...
- ☐ c'est amusant
- ☐ c'est génial
- ☐ c'est difficile
- ☐ ce n'est pas très amusant

construire des maisons,...
- ☐ c'est très amusant
- ☐ c'est agréable
- ☐ c'est facile
- ☐ c'est difficile

danser,...
- ☐ c'est facile
- ☐ c'est assez facile
- ☐ c'est dangereux
- ☐ ce n'est pas très amusant

aller à l'hôpital,...
- ☐ c'est terrible
- ☐ ce n'est pas très amusant
- ☐ c'est intéressant
- ☐ c'est mieux que d'aller dans une navette spatiale

faire du roller,...
- ☐ c'est très facile
- ☐ c'est assez difficile
- ☐ c'est impossible
- ☐ c'est génial

jouer de la guitare,...
- ☐ c'est impossible
- ☐ c'est très difficile
- ☐ c'est super
- ☐ c'est assez amusant

chanter,...
- ☐ c'est difficile
- ☐ c'est mieux que de danser
- ☐ ce n'est pas très amusant
- ☐ c'est assez amusant

Which of the 12 activities do you like best? Put your favourite in the box, and two adjectives in the gaps.

À mon avis, _____ c'est _____ et _____ .